A COMPLEXITY OF EMOTIONS

SILENT DRAFT
ECHOES

101 POEMS

SHEREEN CHRISTINA

INDIA • SINGAPORE • MALAYSIA

ISBN
Paperback 979-8-89699-526-5
Hardcase 979-8-89744-254-6

ABOUT THE AUTHOR

Shereen Christina is a 24-year-old poet—writer who writes about the subtleties of human feeling—confusion, longing, sorrow, and the calm beauty of oddness. Writing turned into her means of understanding a world that too often felt overly noisy, unsettling, unknown, and excessively ordinary. Shereen captures the experience of feeling invisible yet profoundly connected, abandoned, and yearning for belonging in her poetry. Shereen's voice transports readers to a realm where she embraces imperfection and empowers emotions through the intersection of vulnerability and resiliency. When Shereen is not writing, she analyzes the silent occurrences of life that motivate her writing, as she believes poetry has a great ability to provide voice to what remains unspoken. Follow silentdraftechoes on Instagram to connect with Shereen.

ACKNOWLEDGEMENTS

First, to everyone holding this book, thank you for taking a moment to explore these words and emotions.

Thank you, Notion Press Publishing team for believing in this collection, especially Joel Nencil, Rendha Fasil, and Lajja Palaniswamy who were the backbone of making my dream come true.

Thank you, Appa, Amma, Akka, Nehemiah, and Gareb Anne, for believing in me.

Thank you, Shimi, for being my emotional support and existing in my life.

Thank you, Ms. Puspananthiny, for providing a tutorial task that led me to begin writing poems.

Thank you, Karen, for always listening to and reading my random drafts, and being a primary supporter throughout my writing period.

Thank you, Nishalini, Natasha, Amuthan, Sallvina, Thuurgashini, Kanitha, Sivakaarthikkeyen, and Pooja, for being key supporters in my writing journey.

Thank you, Teacher Arutchelvi, for constantly motivating and bringing the best out of me.

Thank you, Ms. Harshreen Kaaur, also known as my 'boss,' for noticing me. You, my boss, made me embrace "oddness", or being different, and I will always cherish being *unusual*. The root of my silent draft—a huge shout-out goes to you, my extraordinary boss!

Above all else, thank you, God. You gave me the courage to share these words.

Thank you to every other person who silently supported me. This book exists because of and for everyone who believes words can connect and heal. I am eternally grateful to each and every soul who played a role in my poetry writing and publishing journey. Each one of you is appreciated; thank you from the bottom of my heart!

*"Poetry is thoughts that breathe,
and words that burn."*

\- Thomas Gray -

odd in an even world

"To find comfort in unspoken words, thoughts, and emotions."

– Shereen Christina –

Silent it was, my draft, yet it echoed.

"*I write only because there is a voice
within me that will not be still*"

– Sylvia Plath –

CONTENTS

CONTENTS

CONTENTS

CONTENTS

CONTENTS

Words—Sword

SHEREEN CHRISTINA
XVIII

#1 FORLORN

Dancing under the stars and draining my soul into the darkness;

The only way to escape is by going through the dark depths of a cave,

Where the light will shine through the shadows.

The last time I touched my heart, I felt the sensation of hurt.

-abandoned

SHEREEN CHRISTINA

#2 MY EYES

My eyes ached and my heart yearns in arrears,

Yearns in arrears to see life clear.

Eyes filled with years of tears,

Years of tears with excessive sears,

Excessive sears bring the sorrow near,

Sorrow nears, but the years of tears and sears fall apart.

My eyes bleed from my sheared heart.

-frozen tears

SHEREEN CHRISTINA

#3 BEZZIES

Moving around with laughter,

Wondering if it would be any better,

Mastering ground with banter,

Holding hands would make it easier,

Whispering sound with a secret power,

Mapping the future if it were closer,

Hiding wounds together,

Wishing it would disappear,

Sharing the soul with a friendship partner,

Hoping it would be forever;

Best of days are always with us,

Escape from our own thoughts,

Zoom in on our memories,

Zero matter of our lives,

Indicate our feelings of love for each other,

Even when our hearts are not at ease,

Soulmates are the best friends we tease,

Keeping us together is the key to our separate journeys.

-we are one

SHEREEN CHRISTINA

#4 INVISIBLE

Investing time alone,

Noticing the value of companionship,

Visualising how it feels to have people around,

Interesting how the feeling is appealing,

Seeing if anyone notices it,

Intimidating how it is not visible to everyone,

Being able to see the fact that it exists,

Lurking in the shadows,

Ending the day, again, knowing I am invisible.

-unnoticed

SHEREEN CHRISTINA

#5 RECOGNITION

The first fierce look,

The strange sweet connection,

Like I have known you since the beginning of birth,

Like we share a common bond,

The care to fill eternal emptiness,

The love of your heart is a great gift,

Like the gentle grace you have offered,

Like the keen kindness you have given,

The genuine generosity that comes through your presence is a testament to the strength and resilience you possess in this life,

The first fierce look of yours reflects the spirit that has always existed, like a light that shines through the darkness from your soul;

Connection, happiness, exhilaration, and reverence from recognition.

-soulmate

SHEREEN CHRISTINA

#6 HOURS OF DARKNESS

The quiet world in the hours of darkness,

Pondering under the black skies,

Where my shadow abandons me,

The shadow that will never be seen.

The darkness that comes through my soul,

Questioning the running sounds in my mind,

Wondering what the world is like without darkness.

The world is indeed full of darkness that can be seen.

The loud mind, with the war of words,

Begging the mind to be at peace,

Throwbacks to the uncomfortable reality,

Hits from the realistic world of chaos,

The dying inner soul that has been lost in memory;

From soul to mind and mind to soul in the hours of
darkness.

-blackout

SHEREEN CHRISTINA

#7 FAZE

Smiling through the rain,

The rain that conceals pain.

Heading into the hurricane,

The hurricane that drives insane.

Excruciating feelings of despair;

The despair that leads to being impair.

Rewinding the unsaid thoughts,

The thoughts that never have retorts.

Evolving into an endless route,

The route that led to being mute.

Emptying the path to a new territory,

The territory that has been an allegory.

Noticing the present moment,

The moment that is silent.

Similar to a promise that ends and the wishes that
never come true, the faze seed unnerves.

–disturbed

SHEREEN CHRISTINA

#8 IN SILENCE

In silence,

She was in her own zone,

The zone where her introspections hone.

In silence,

She was able to see her spark,

The spark that hides her dark.

In silence,

She felt the ache of being lost,

The lost spirit that was gliding like a ghost.

In silence,

She felt her own existence,

The existence that was vanishing became non-existence.

In silence,

She accepted the reality.

The reality of the uproar in her mind that she is still trying to escape from, her mentality.

In silence, the voice of her thoughts echoed the loudest, causing violence in her head.

In silence,

She comforted her restless soul.

In silence.

-she

SHEREEN CHRISTINA

#9 NATURE

Human nature is to seek Mother Nature when human nature is overwhelmed by its own nature.

Mother Nature speaks in a way that human nature feels at home, where the human mind can be at ease and at peace.

The landscape of emotions between Mother Nature and human nature is a reminder of the beauty to be found within nature.

-raw beauty

SHEREEN CHRISTINA

#10 PAWFECT LOVE

My heart skips a beat when your eyes gaze,

Yet the words fall into place.

Sometimes I wonder if you understand words,

Hoping to convey my hurts.

In every situation to keep me whole,

Mother who consoles,

Image of my soul.

Grumpy at times,

It's a way of feeling annoyed sometimes.

Runs and climbs,

Love, that rhymes.

Leaving your scent in my heart,

Oh, my love, you are an art.

Voiceless soul that plays a huge part,

Even if you cannot see the impart,

Never depart.

-pet, shimi

#11 THE DUSK

The dusk,

The day before dawn,

The last time the sun was out for the day,

The dark shades dominate the colours of the sky,

Reminding one that the day is about to end,

Bringing the fear of darkness into the night.

Even though the colours could be pretty at first,

It was going to bring darkness,

The darkness that intimidates.

The hope of seeing a new day is not certain,

The uncertainties of witnessing the bright ray,
because of the growing darkness.

Dusk isn't a choice but a duress to catch sight of.

Dusk,

The beautiful colours fade away as the day wears on,
reminding us that everything comes to an end despite
being beautiful.

The quick transition of sunsets gives way to the long
dawn lights, bringing hope in the form of varying
stunning blues throughout the day.

The dusk,

Simply unsettling, and it fades away in no time.

–sunset

SHEREEN CHRISTIN

#12 MY FOUNDATION

Thank you, my life's glue.

Freedom and trust grew,

You never rushed me through.

Blind faith that you bestowed,

Always empowered and overflowed.

I am eternally grateful,

You gave me a plateful.

Thank you, you two.

I am who I am due to both of you.

-pa and ma

SHEREEN CHRISTINA

#13 ABOVE AND BELOW

The sky and the sea.
Everyone is so busy looking forward that one overlooks
what is above and below in this world of beauty.
Ever wonder?
If the sky and sea resemble each other,
If the sky and sea depths are equal,
If the sky's clouds and the sea's creatures could be the same,
If the sky rains and sea floods are similar,
If the sky falls and the sea rise are mirroring their natural
appearance.
The sky's weaving clouds and the sea's waves are the
throwing back of above and below.
Both blues slowly stir around in their own directions,
Ensuring their rhythmic tales are not a forgotten action.
The sky and sea have beauty to be seen that is identical
in every aspect if one tilts their head above and below to
see them instead of just looking forward for the common
sight.
Isn't everyone just looking at something ordinary?
That they forget one is not made for the common but to
embrace the uniqueness of oneself along with the world
around them.
Something as simple as the sky and sea is the most
beautiful reflection one could witness.
Simple yet often pleasing to the eyes.
The human eyes are most striking when they are drawn to
the sky and sea.
The eyes are where the waves reflect from above and
below.
The vast sky and the intense sea—did you notice them?

-the blues

SHEREEN CHRISTINA
26

#14 FLOOD

Invisibility of wind that brushes hair,

Hair sways while the sun kisses the face,

Face glows in the daylight in eyes,

Eyes shine with a captivating smile,

Smile enchantingly while the world gazes at the beautiful appearance,

Appearance that buries emotions well,

The emotions that make up the body,

The body that holds them together is the soul,

The soul, which prevents the heart and mind from breaking down into pieces of flesh,

The flesh that is broken by the invisible force of nature,

Nature triggers a reality check on feelings,

The feelings that always choose to flood in stillness,

Stillness that will never end in tears but in the shears of a heart,

And the heart conceals every distress by displaying a beautiful look to the world.

The world cherishes the beauty of the human body and the invisibility of the inner soul.

Take a bow, unhappy souls with the most precious look.

-covered emotions

SHEREEN CHRISTINA

#15 DEFEATED

The twists of a confused cerebration,

In the midst of a crushed aspiration,

The mind that strays from motivation,

In a war zone of excruciating imagination,

Fighting the battle for freedom from mental tribulation,

Emotions that echo frustration,

Feeling of numbness in isolation,

Choking pain of word's rejection,

Defeated by a force of unspoken hesitation.

-unvoiced

SHEREEN CHRISTINA

#16 UNBROKEN

The make-up is shaded with colour powder,

Blinding lights at the edges of the further,

Roaming of the miseries whispers,

Overwhelming the masked breather,

Keeping the veil on to be an avoider,

Ensuring everything is shadowy from others,

Needing no aid to be a pretender,

Putting the pieces together, being unbroken to not bother.

-in one piece

#17 EYES

The twisting tale of it,

Hides hurt from the shoreline,

Speaking volumes vehemently, yet it is still silent,

Ever seen the aesthetic art in the eyes?

Yearning to be naturally noticed,

Every time it says something complex,

Strangely, the eyes play tricks,

Leaving wrinkles from a sore smile,

Distracting others from looking long at it,

Guessing the eyes echo truly,

Because it acts amazingly well.

An intense emotion beneath the eyes.

Indeed, eyes do not lie; they manipulate.

-steering look

SHEREEN CHRISTINA

#18 UPROAR

Noise! Noise!

The surroundings are loud.

It disturbs my thinking.

How do I cope with such an inconvenience?

Or is it the noise in my head?

Causing irritation to the mind.

Between the confusion of my thoughts and the backspaced words,

The uncommon sense of the word was not enough for the listener to grasp the meaning behind it.

So, it causes the noise of chatter in the mind.

Discussing the conversation within my own mind.

The noises are just another usual thing that happens.

Yet it is unsettling – the noise.

-disruption

SHEREEN CHRISTINA

#19 FRAME OF MIND

Midst of a long everyday battle,

Oceans of rides throughout the day,

Overflowing of the swings,

Discovery of spinning tempers,

The invisibility of shifting moods within the mind.

-mood

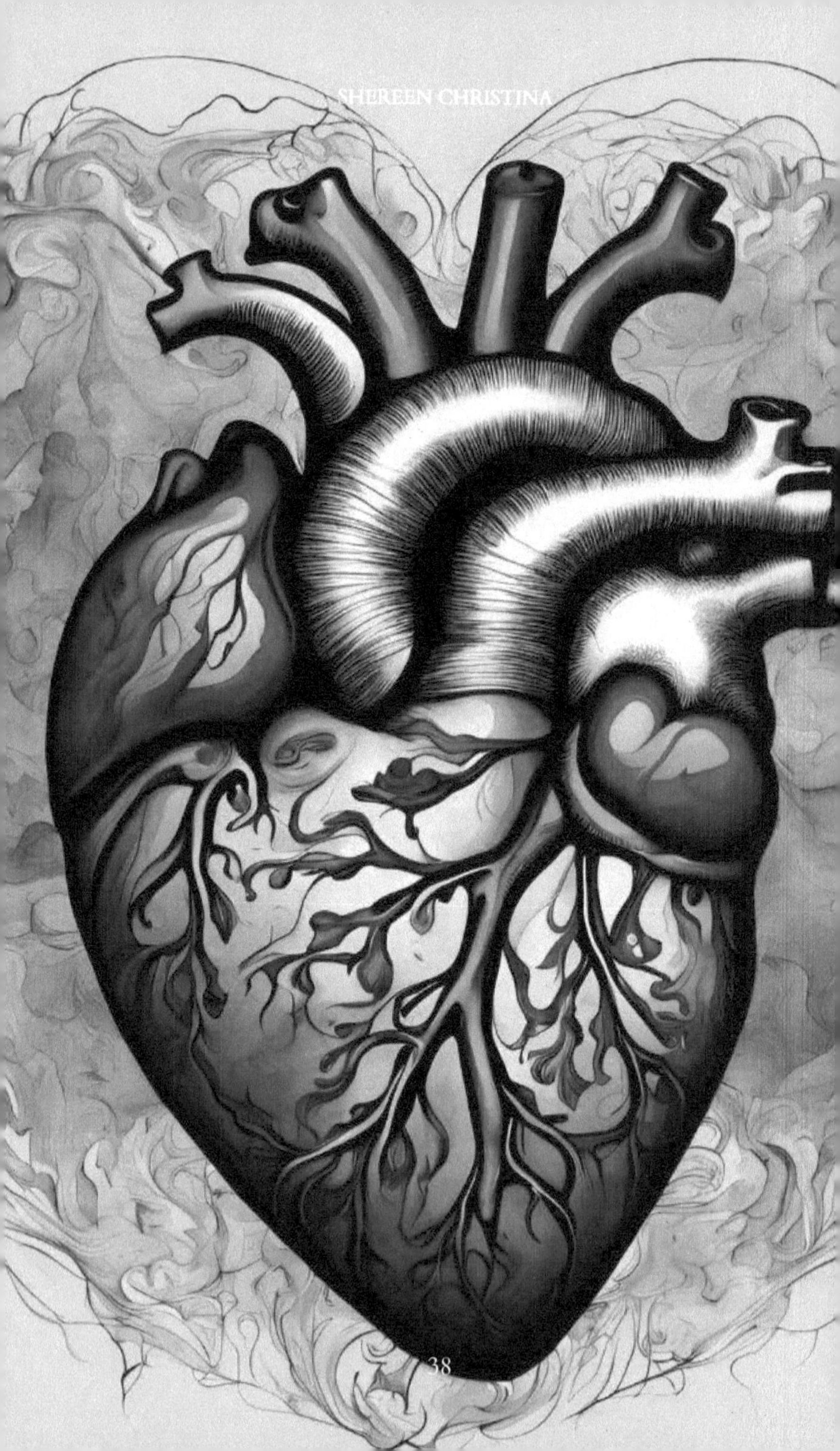
SHEREEN CHRISTINA
38

#20 HEART

He is an art,

Evenly written by the artist,

Amazes the surrounding landscape,

Revealing the inner voice with the eyes,

Touching souls with love,

He is an art, the heart.

-inside art

SHEREEN CHRISTINA

#21 REMEMBRANCE

It still rings,

The words that sting.

Though something in me died on the twelfth,

Yet the words live in every breath.

It never stopped haunting the mind until today.

Why couldn't it slip away?

The words that pierced my soul in every way,

You make me feel grey day-to-day because of the painful say,

And now it will always stay,

An excruciating memory that I pay a visit to every day.

-words

SHEREEN CHRISTINA
42

#22 UNUSUAL

Mystery or misery,

Silence of trickery.

Uniqueness that works as a threat to others,

Never relating everything to anything in colours.

Unevenly existing,

Suppress the odd ducks in the world of common consisting.

Uncommon intimidates,

Always crazy to the eyes of imitates.

Leaving ordinary's most appealing,

Strange souls are invisible's dreaming.

Callings of 'difficult' rather than different,

Unusually usual, the contrastive magnificent.

-offbeat

#23 FIRE UP

Making sure never to be ordinary,

Spotting the extraordinary.

Here and there with a little hurry,

Aware of every soul in summary.

Right on the edge ground,

Spilling the mysterious aura around,

Heading towards the sound.

Resembling the light of a fire,

Emerging force of desire.

Even in exhausting situations,

Never to lose determination.

Tuning out the motivation,

Yet inspiring future generations.

A fire to view,

See your value,

Never leave it behind you.

-boss

SHEREEN CHRISTINA

#24 MOVE

The first sight of hope, when the eyes met,

Overwhelming emotions in the heart's depth.

The connection between, like no other,

Sudden drifting in a direction that feels unreal to suffer.

The hope ruptured, as did the intimidating thought of being trapped in my own mind,

Own mind that chooses to live with delusional thoughts that blind.

The thoughts that interrupt from moving forward,

Stuck in the corner with words.

Waiting for the hope to be fulfilled, found or destroyed,

The possibility that it was almost there was never void.

Hope crumbles rapidly,

Indelible scars on individuality.

–one sided

SHEREEN CHRISTINA

#25 SOLITUDE

The quietest of nights,

Where being alone feels lonelier,

The empty presence of loneliness makes it hard to find peace.

Though the isolation is a constant reminder of what it feels like to be alive yet dead,

It is the withdrawal of the soul that is causing the death of the human while we live on.

The desire to be alone has waned,

Slipping away from the silent side,

Heading towards the noise,

Escaping an eruption of emotions,

Running away from solitude in the midst of darkness and fear of quietness.

Sometimes evenly existing can be extremely exhausting.

-withdrawal

#26 WALL OF THOUGHTS

Caught myself staring at the wall.

The wall was mirroring thoughts,

Ever wondered how a wall could mirror thoughts?

It wasn't about the wall but the way it was made,

Just like the thoughts,

Covered with paint to keep the rawness from becoming visible.

The rawness isn't appealing or attractive to the naked eye, so it must be concealed.

Look at the wall and listen to what it says about the stares it gets,

It probably mirrors the thoughts of the people who watched it for a long time,

Feeling blue for their ponder.

The thoughts that were never heard and ran tirelessly,

The wall witnessed it all, the swirling thoughts.

Indeed, I was staring at the wall of thoughts.

-reflection

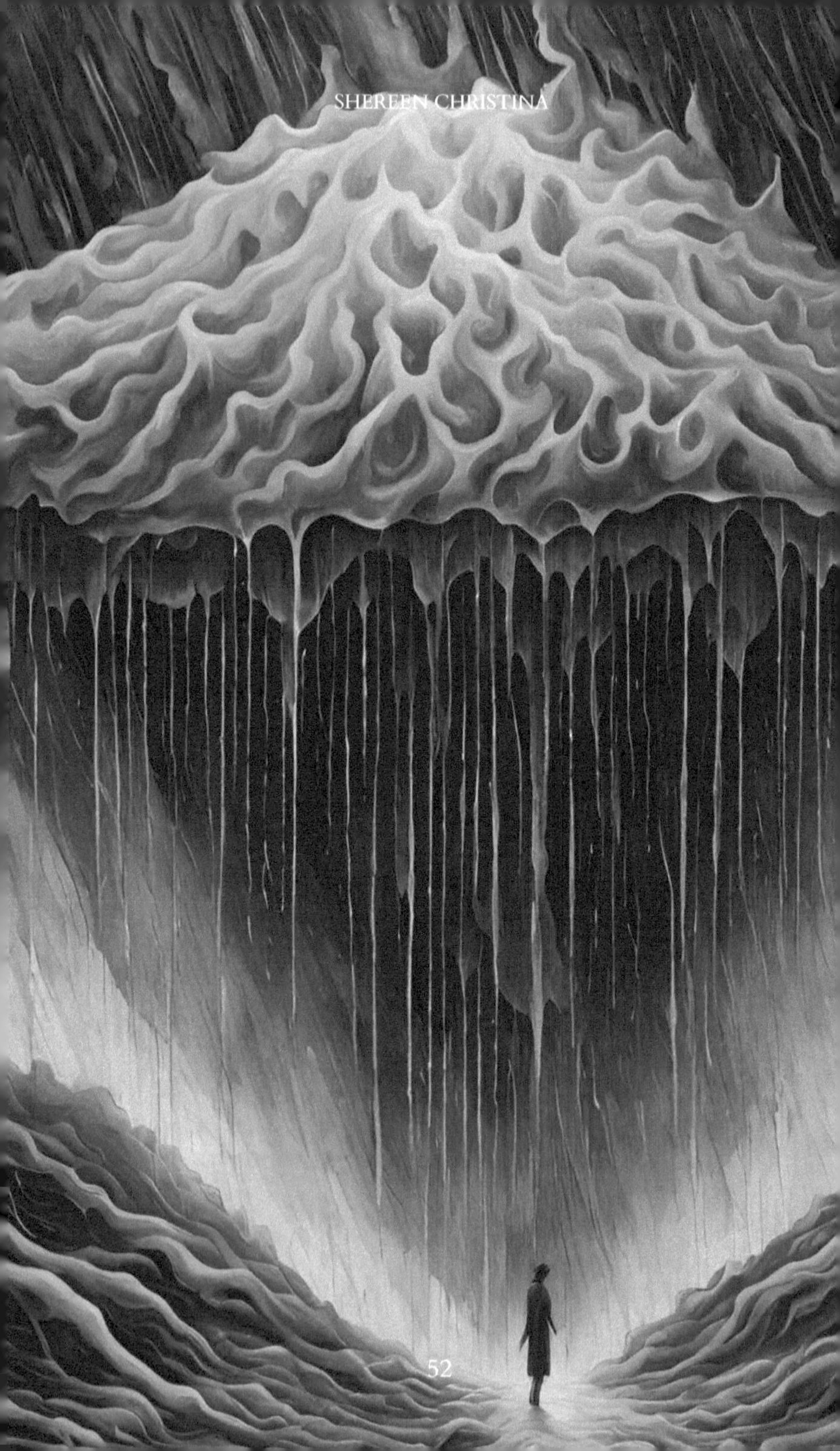
SHEREEN CHRISTINA
SHEREEN CHRISTINA
52

#27 PAIN

Pouring rain from the wounds,

Aching of the heart is intense;

Inevitable sting from soreness,

Never-ending misery from brokenness.

Need no words to express,

It is similar to being cold,

Armed the soul,

Protecting myself from the world.

To keep pain in words, not to be heard.

−misery

SHEREEN CHRISTINA

#28 MOMENT

The scraps of time that are left in the dust will fade into a dull grey sky,

Leaving the hope high,

Questioning why?

Just like a moment that slips away, blurry,

The good times fall apart in a hurry,

Leaving sour ones lingering long in worry,

The moment that intimidates without sorry, in memory.

−story of a moment

SHEREEN CHRISTINA

#29 MOON AND SUN

Why is the moon cherished and the sun ignored?

Many take pictures of the moon.

And what about the sun?

Shining from darkness is cool,

How about being a light amidst the brightness?

Perhaps being a constant gets you overlooked,

And being irregularly in distant creates space for appreciation, although it is not consistent.

The tale of being an existence.

-neglection

#30 GLOAMING HOPE

Patiently awaiting the fading bright,

Meanwhile, the sun plays a part in the stage of light,

From the vanishing of blue to gold sight,

The thoughts ponder a little more in tight,

Silently cherishing the transition with delight,

Hoping the writes bring a better tonight,

And rewrites for tomorrow to be alright.

-evening dream

SHEREEN CHRISTINA
60

#31 BELIEVE

Building a new hope into each day,

Every day is a reminder to make it through,

Leaving behind the doubts, stray,

Immense emotions that never felt true,

Every now and then, but never left the queue.

Voice of the void amidst the light,

Echoing through the night.

The hope that gives relief,

Never to leave,

And on every eve, I believe.

−count on

SHEREEN CHRISTINA

#32 DISTRESS

Like the last tick of the day,

The tears are always on the verge of a falling way.

Eyes have never been obvious to the crowd,

The untruth lies between the clouds.

Away goes the silent ache,

The secrets beneath the shadows shake.

Voiceless and mysterious,

The darkness from weariness.

Every dusk with fears,

The eyes remain open with tears.

-holding on

SHEREEN CHRISTINA

#33 CHAOS

Turn of lefts and rights,

Rushing the lane to reach the end of the maze of traffic lights.

Around the clock and then running back,

Floating on the ground to not lack.

Falling in the air of a daydream,

It is a way to escape the stream,

Chaos! The scream from the extreme.

–traffic madness

SHEREEN CHRISTINA

#34 INSECURE

Isolation behind the lens of the world,

Nightmares of self-doubt swirl.

Somewhere in between the storm,

Endless truth lies beneath the clouds' form.

Cold air numbs the soul tight,

Unsure of existence in the light.

Right in consciousness,

Every uncertainty echoes the insecureness.

-self-conscious

SHEREEN CHRISTINA

#35 COFFEE

Black and white, the vague soul,

In time, it is hot and ice cold.

Trick of the bold,

To avoid anxious sounds, control.

Every sip to uphold,

Running away from the untold.

Black and bitter, gold will never get old.

Black and bitter gold...

Do I have it? Yes, though.

Do I like it? Sometimes, oh, or no—

Do I enjoy it? Somewhat, so.

Do I need it? Surely! To go.

-black soul, black coffee

SHEREEN CHRISTINA

#36 DOUBTFUL

Drifting through the beliefs of my own,

Odd, the things that cross my mind's zone,

Unknown to the rest of my known.

Blurry tones,

Triggers the usual stones,

Force of ache in my bone,

Unclear mind that haunts my throne,

Lurking, the voice in my head as my body moves
forward alone.

-unsettling mind

#37 GREY

Soo grey,

The way,

Maybe it is a display,

That it will be a good day,

Starting from an unclear ray,

To see the light today,

Grey but not dark way.

-dull not dark

SHEREEN CHRISTINA

#38 SKY

The sun is out,

And so are the clouds.

The bright sky that leaves no doubt,

Every shade that roams about,

To be seen throughout.

Even when the wind shouts,

The sky remains proud and beautifully loud.

-the vast blue

SHEREEN CHRISTINA

#39 LONER

Lies within the walls of my head,

Oceans of thoughts trying to escape the dark gate,

Never-ending ink words of red,

Endless wrenching pain that is a threat,

Leaving marks of the unsaid,

Yet a forlorn is never dead but waits to be aid.

-lonely

SHEREEN CHRISTINA
78

#40 MOTHER NATURE

New views to gaze at,

Every landscape takes the breath away, in fact.

Wind that blows through the mountain's breath,

Zeal for peace to the mind's depth.

Epic and beautiful in every display,

Art, the Mother Nature's way.

Long rides remind the value of aesthetics,

Awaken the poetics.

Nights of quiet and cold air rise,

Days in chill winds and calm skies.

-new zealand

#41 FIRST

Ought to be a waymaker,

Leaving behind all self-worth that awakens her.

Dreams of the cageless sense of being,

Even in the midst of chaos, bleeding,

Races the mind to thinking,

Creating an everlasting wound for healing,

Hoping for some fresh breathing,

Intimidation of expectations is screaming,

Letting go every minute to pleasing,

Dream, dream of a day for self-wellbeing.

-first born

SHEREEN CHRISTINA
82

#42 MUSIC

Moving sounds that distract ringing,

Unreal at times of drowning.

Speak volumes to quiet the mind,

In a moment of calm, kind.

Caressing the pain and suffering,

Music, the mesmerising way of nurturing.

-calming tones

SHEREEN CHRISTINA

#43 YLENOL

Loneliness eats me bit by bit.

I did not realise until I saw parts of me were being a missing fit.

Some were crying, "Submit!"

And others were screaming, "Quit!"

Year by year, month by month, week by week,

Day by day, hour by hour, minute by minute, second by second,

Solitude begins to be a threat with no end,

And never left a door unlocked to escape the bend.

Every moment that engulfs my mind,

From beginning to end in an intimidating line.

The sense of fear trembles my body in whole.

Please! Please! Please! Begged the soul.

-all alone

SHEREEN CHRISTINA

#44 WIND

Blows in ease,

The air breeze,

And the wind that calms my mind, at least.

Though hair curls in a wave to tease,

The mess claims no fees.

It is one of the most common keys,

To deliver the invisible kiss,

That never fails to please.

Instead, the moving mystery sees,

In a way that makes me freeze.

And then it flees.

-twist and turn

#45 ACHE

The indescribable sentiment of the deep sea,

Shallow to the eyes of thee.

Waves of struggling air in tense introspection,

Attack of a thousand stone collection,

Leaving each one to haunt in every direction,

Leading to an explosion of emotions and resurrection,

Ordinary and common to form the connection,

Writing the motion of a deep-sea reflection,

That seems shallow but actually swallows the whole body with the perfection of rejection.

-suffering

SHEREEN CHRISTINA

#46 THIRD

Young to be the best,

Old soul in test.

Unexpressed voice that makes a request,

Never seriously to be addressed.

Growing in the moment of freedom,

Eternal road of a peaceful museum.

Slips and shadows of a distant future,

Troubles the youthful mind sooner.

-youngest child

#47 STORMY

Self-discovering,

Every uttering,

The head buffering,

In every suffering,

Emotions too shattering,

The pain of recovering,

Smile to colour the acting,

Every day I am hurting.

Stuttering in the midst of a storming,

The ache that comes with thundering.

-internal chaos

SHEREEN CHRISTINA

#48 BLOOM

Unseen by many friendlies,

Now or never in the twenties.

Noise of an explosion in silence,

Old phase to guidance.

Through the dark maze to blooming,

In the path that is tuning,

Carrying hope of improving.

Eyes on the sky with a smile,

Dials day and night in style to go the extra mile for
the inner child.

-hopeful invisible

SHEREEN CHRISTINA

#49 WHY ME?

Looked above and saw Your grace,

Wonder if I ever deserve any of the embrace.

You make me smile in my darkest moments of life,

Finding a way through to the light, to strive.

Joy and peace, You are in my mind,

Every moment with You heals me fine.

Soul that eases my heart,

Unsung Hero, who helps my shattered shadow
depart,

Spirit of love that sees and comforts me in every part,

Every day You make me ponder in art, why me?

-God

#50 WRITE

Words, words and words.
Write, write and write.

Word. Words.
Rewrites the entire lines of misery stirred,
Ironically, it is always left unheard.
Torment at the end of every page,
Emotions in the cage.

Write. Writes.
Rewords the unusual and unspoken thoughts,
Inside a mind report.
Turbulence in the heart,
Evokes heavy art.
Writing, the profound sense of words part.

Words in writing are not just a form of expression
but an art that has been translated into the inked
blood.

-commit to paper

SHEREEN CHRISTINA

#51 DESIRE

I wish I wish you had spoken more to me,

It may have made a difference to me,

Though you exist, I wish you were free,

To hear all I see, I charge no fee,

Yet you become an absentee,

I guarantee that I am not an ordinary tree,

But a deep sea,

Wishing to have foreseen, before I flee,

Oh! Maybe I should have made a plea to notice me!

-yearning

SHEREEN CHRISTINA

#52 SECOND

The average soul in a complex world,

Hanging on the comparison whirled.

Every night, the words came to live,

Mysterious to the pounding of life.

Ice-cold soul on the edge of the knife,

Dark and tough on a daily drive.

Dead in the silence of an intense storm,

Light that is never warm.

Echoing a distant sound from the mind,

Coping within the spot of the blind.

Happiness that temporarily follows behind,

Irritation that usually left declined.

Leaving each unsaid word to bury,

Dusting the truth of scary to hide the worry,

Middle and second to every other story,

Iron heart that seeks to heal in a hurry.

Sense of being unheard and unseen in all ways,

Erupts the ache in the shattered peace maze,

Repeats a story of the past phases that faze,

Yearning to be visible in every gaze and every breath
of the day.

-middle child

SHEREEN CHRISTINA

#53 AGONY

Terrifying, the head,

Outplays of words said.

Rough and tough, the voices of my thoughts,

Marks that leave me lost.

Electrifying, the way I feel,

Nights of war to deal,

Torture to heal.

Agony! Agony! The darkness reveals.

−torment

#54 CLOUD

Certainly not aware,

Lurking around here and there,

Oh, you are not consistent anywhere,

Using your own rhythms to ponder everywhere,

Delight with every glare,

Swirling around in your way of fair,

Yet you are still the visible one that gets an unnoticed stare.

-visibly invisible

SHEREEN CHRISTINA

#55 MASKED

Under the shadowed act,

Never seen, in fact.

Siren head that echoes silent drafts,

Elevates the written craft.

Even in a crowd,

Noise of thoughts roars loud.

Switching of display,

Claims to be the way of everyday,

The concealed sorrow beneath the smile's sway.

—secret sense

SHEREEN CHRISTINA

#56 HOPE

The hope for quiet and calmness,

Haunts me in my oddness.

Utterly shattered by thoughts,

Nomad of my force.

Down, the head falls deep down,

Errors in my mind abound.

Rough, the holding up,

In every place, disrupt.

Noises, the madness of day and night,

Glazes the air with some light to write, right!

−desire

SHEREEN CHRISTINA

#57 LIGHT

Just when I thought there was no light,

Whispers of "you are a colourful kite,"

Free in its own way of delight,

Darkness surrounds; to ensure you are bright,

Visible to the similar sights,

Smile through the sting of the bite,

Keep moving; there is always a fight for better nights.

-motivation

#58 UNKNOWN

Look around, take a moment to inhale,

The surroundings that could alleviate the torment scale,

Notice the tiny details,

It isn't just tales,

But the emotion that sails,

Exhale the fails,

Unknown rails unveil new ways!

−mystery

SHEREEN CHRISTINA

#59 CHILDHOOD

Chased by eagerness to escape the tranquillity of peace,

Never realising it strips the soul's ease.

Wishing to move backwards,

Now that everything makes me feel like a coward,

Forward, forward, yells grown-up words.

Sometimes, I wish I savoured the moments of childhood,

Before it became one that I cannot reach out for good.

-good old days

#60 UNCOMMON

Everyone seemed to be aware of life's route,

While I am stuck in my chaotic suit.

Unable to see the usual way of living,

Freeze in my own being.

Common, the human thinking,

Lost, the unusual mind in an attempt to fit in.

-non-ordinary human

SHEREEN CHRISTINA

#61 WISHFUL

Lost in my own world of yearning,

Oh, how I am invisibly craving?

Nightmares of my unheard voice lingering,

Gagging, the words of hankering.

Infinite hope to crumble,

Noises that stumble,

God! I am a trouble!

-longing

#62 UNEASE

My hands; they are cold,

And my soul is old,

Oh, my feet cannot be on hold,

It vibrates according to my mind's control,

The head races to uphold,

And I try to stroll and withhold,

Behold! Behold!

I console myself to be bold.

-anxiety

SHEREEN CHRISTINA

#63 STRUGGLE

I struggle mentally,

But oh, it must not be said so eventually,

The crowd whispers generally,

That everyone goes through it, potentially,

So, the struggles are just common usually,

And my mental state does not matter sentimentally.

Here it goes, the war of my identity,

Exposing the mentality,

That doesn't make sense to anybody.

–depressed

SHEREEN CHRISTINA

#64 SORE

Bruises of damage,

Rises in every age,

Oh, I must manage!

Known rage,

Engage strange,

New page leads to uncertain change,

And stillness in a cage stage.

-brokenness

STEEN CHRISTINA

#65 MISSED

Running away from chances,

Every moment that could have been the answer,

Game of life that dances,

Reimagining pieces left, like glasses,

Each part of life, like branches,

Taking a diversion to the past and future but never to be the present timers.

Down it goes, opportunities that were left behind because of unsureness.

−regret

SHEREEN CHRISTINA

#66 YEAR

Oh! It is December, but I forgot to flip the calendar.

It's the year-end, and I am still thinking of January
that hides under,

February that went by in top gear,

March that marched unclear,

The April that did not quite fool anyone this year,
being a balancer,

May that may have been a stir,

June reminds me that I am halfway through the year,

July held a web of chaotic emotions here.

It is almost done for the year...

But I am still in August, that gust of fears,

September that was shadowy and severe,

Oh, October, that reminds me of mental troubles
with sincere,

November that nobody noticed the year-end is near,

And now, December is here to disappear,

Knocking on January to reappear.

-year closure

#67 OKAY

Somewhere in between, I saw myself fading,

Fading of my actual self into shading, shading of covering in fact.

The realisation that never stopped echoing through the day,

Day with the light to have its say,

And nights when the silence haunts me until I lay.

Am I even myself? Doubt that always stays, never goes away.

How can I display? Being a ray or grey, the mind delays.

I am okay, I say, at least for today, not to decay.

—not okay

SHEREEN CHRISTINA

#68 MIND

Maybe, maybe I cannot fit in,

Inside my head, the echoes take a spin.

Need not be perfect,

Dynamic voice to protect,

Mind machine that directs,

Aims to control the indirect.

Causing chaos at times,

Hoping the spirit stays in rhyme,

Immersing in a whirlwind of emotions that blind,

New and valid, the soul reminds,

Echoing mind, you are surely one of a kind!

-inside out

SHEREEN CHRISTINA

#69 BLUES

Sometimes,

Just sometimes,

It rhymes,

The emotion that wishes to commit crimes,

But instead, the words take a stand and climb,

Replacing the soul between the lines,

Leaving no signs, nor fines,

Yet it declines,

The feeling to shine,

Will I ever be fine?

The sounds from my mind.

-sorrow echoes

#70 DRAFT

Muted the inside rings,

Yet it stings.

Swaying between the pages,

Illusion, at times the phrases,

Lost at well-known places,

Era of dark phases,

Notion for new spaces;

Torment that leaves traces,

Dream of changes.

Random writings to revive,

And to survive,

Feels alive.

The words that glide through my head,

Empties the soul – dead.

Chaotic and messy in drafts,

Hurricanes that cause mind blasts.

Oh, but outside, yellowed,

Emotions that are narrowed,

Silent it was, my draft, yet it echoed.

-quiet writing reflects

#71 IMPERFECT

Confusion or conclusion,

The way of poetic imperfection,

Is there even perfection?

Phrases that are written in delusion,

Haunts every possible solution,

Cursed, the words of true emotion,

Bleeding from the chaotic inside eruptions,

That leaves no trace of soul in motion.

So, it is indeed the perfection of imperfection.

-accept flaws

SHEREEN CHRISTINA

#72 FLOAT

It's 2:32 am, but the clouds are visibly hanging in the sky.

Just like my emotions that are peaking high.

Uttering in silence, that echo my inner voices,

Oh, maybe it rejoices to appear with choices.

Why doesn't it disappear along with the darkness?

Being a disruptive force in the world of quietness,

Reminding it to fade away in stillness,

Yet, its madness sounds as harshness,

The clouds, the feelings, float in invisibleness,

Waiting to fall apart before the sun rises.

-pondering emotions

#73 UNCLEAR

Urge of my ache,

Never to brake,

Keeping it together for the sake,

Nerves that shake,

Order to break,

Wish to wake,

Now that my ache yells, mistake! Mistake!

-known emotions

#74 BIRTHDAY

The anxiety before a birthday,

Where time crawls,

As the clock ticks on the wall.

The uncertainty during a birthday,

Where the rain showers throughout the day.

The stormy night reflecting new ways,

And hope of rays,

To be the light of my every day.

The ignorance after the birthday,

Just another day, says a soul that wishes it were more
than just a day.

Again, back to the reality of being a stray,

But my pen and papers stay and never betray.

-one day celebrity

#75 FOGGY

Cloudy minds,

Loud voices,

Odd whirlwinds,

Unclear messages,

Desperate wounds,

Yell damages.

-cloudy emotions

SHEREEN CHRISTINA

#76 MISSION

I speak in poetry every day,

But nobody listens to anything that I convey,

Only to shut out the truth that stiffens,

Yet I was on a mission,

The drafts to bring my vision!

-lone wolf

SHEREEN CHRISTINA

#77 BOND

How does the human mind work?

My pondering that lurks.

Searching for connections that share similar traits,

To never have common debates, but to unusually relate.

The relevance of the extraordinary creates,

To the human mind, weights.

So, I await an uncommon tie that will **rate** my narrates.

-likewise soul

SHEREEN CHRISTINA

#78 SHE

She hides her glowy sides,

And it slowly slides, the way she talks about her insides.

In every ride, she smiles to keep her sorrows aside,

She lied to every console that came to her side,

The wide crowd that usually never replied,

Curious to provide, though she denied,

And she shows pride in the attention she never applied.

She tried and cried,

And died by her own words of fights.

-avoidance kills

SHEREEN CHRISTINA

#79 HIDDEN

I am merely an existent,

That waits to be seen in a distant,

Never in anyone's radar of consistent,

Yes, I exist but as insufficient.

-overlooked

#80 PLEA

I did not realise what pain was,

Until I was on my knees,

Begging God for memory loss,

To erase all the aching pain in my head.

Oh, how deeply I did not want to remember
anything but forget everything.

-falling apart

SHEREEN CHRISTINA

#81 POETRY

Poetry, a beautiful language built,

Though many don't comprehend it.

Yet the words are there,

Somewhere in the air.

Between the lines of my soundless pages,

Or maybe it roars in empty places,

In every age and phase,

The words swirl for changes.

-poems

SHEREEN CHRISTINA

#82 UNINTERESTED

And suddenly, I lost interest in all the things I once loved doing.

I even fall asleep quickly,

Before falling apart in my mind, sickly.

Is this being numb or dumb?

Perhaps this is what I have become,

Someone who has scattered like crumbs.

-unfeeling

SHEREEN CHRISTINA

#83 MISUSE

People, people, cool!

Strange, I was used as a stepping stool.

Oh, I was merely a tool,

What a fool!

Dreadfully painful,

The way of life rules.

-play on

SHEREEN CHRISTINA

#84 UNSAID

Unreal and unsettling,

Now or never in my mind's lettering.

Swell eyes with the words of the untold,

And heart with a smile of cold,

Deep breath to behold,

The intense weight of unvoiced longs to unfold.

-suppressed

#85 FROZEN

Woken,

To be unbroken,

Weight of the unspoken,

Here and there, yet always frozen.

Emotions, never in motion,

Thoughts of explosion, am I chosen?

-iced doubts

#86 NUMB

I cannot cry, though I try,

Maybe I am numb; that is why.

Always low and never high,

The feelings that never reply.

Covering by being shy,

And deny not to rely,

Goodbye, the emotions that always underly.

-emotion paralyzed

SHEREEN CHRISTINA

#87 REJECTION

Nobody listens to my definitions,

Maybe I am not everybody's choice of edition,

Being a different version with an unusual vision,

People want me an omission because of my intuitions,

I guess I belong in a prison of cognitions that meets my condition.

-being different

SHEREEN CHRISTINA
174

#88 HOPELESS

Dreaming of the days of freedom,

Eagerly awaiting the empty museum.

Slowly but surely, the headache echoes,

Planting hopes of a clear mind flow.

Am I going to make it?

Inside the head, calling it quits.

Rough and tough, I admit.

—museum mind

SHEREEN CHRISTINA

#89 NO LOVE

The love that I did not receive,

Come expectantly to perceive.

Will it be a relief?

Oh, I do not believe.

Leave! Leave!

Let me grieve.

The world that deceives, no need to retrieve.

I am not naive, but here to achieve, though no love weaved.

-solitary

SHEREEN CHRISTINA

#90 MIND AND HEART

I thought my mind was in a war zone,

In reality, it is the heart that becomes heavy on its own.

My mind, tortured with thoughts,

My heart, pierced with painful force.

The mind still could think freely,

Except my heart stopped letting feelings in easily.

Perhaps it is not the mind that is excruciating,

But the heart that quits feeling for anything.

The mind plays hard, only to hurt the heart.

My mind, a chaos that binds with the heart to remind the ache left behind.

-loud mind haunts silent heart

#91 YOU

Look at you, sacrificing your life,

For the surrounding souls to survive and thrive.

Will it be enough?

Your routine—that is rough.

Wake up! Wake up!

It is not a dream, so interrupt!

Your spirit awaits your genuine desires,

See what it requires and fuel it with fire before you expire.

–self-love

SHEREEN CHRISTINA

#92 MONDAY

Monday motivation, they say,

The Monday that makes everyone run away,

I wonder how it is even a day,

Either way, I do not want to stay,

Can I just lay?

Delay today for a while until I feel okay,

Oh! Monday makes me feel grey.

-Monday blues

SHEREEN CHRISTINA

#93 ONE DAY

I mould myself a little, like clay,

The cold years took a toll to portray,

I am not gold on display,

The old me still looks for a way,

I hold myself with the weights every day,

The controlled mind buffers until today,

And hopes to be bold someday,

Can I escape one day?

-hopeful change

SHEREEN CHRISTINA
186

#94 NEVER ENOUGH

Day and night of hustle to waste,

Imperfection of day-to-day life in a place,

Since the beginning to the end of an effort to base,

Anchoring each day with a new strength of blaze,

Pushing the balance in haste,

Plotting the path for improvement in the maze,

Outlining an action to outshine in every phase,

Immersing in the process of transformation with grace,

Not realising the evolution will be inadequate for the race,

The feeling of lacking everything seals the belief in a daze,

The sting marks will exist for an eternity, even if I ace,

Never enough, as always.

-insufficient

SHEREEN CHRISTINA

#95 THREATENING PRECISION

Maybe I should not aim for perfection that ruins my head,

The anxiety that shoots up as a threat.

Almost dead! Almost dead!

I nearly lost myself instead,

The mind that always thinks ahead.

Though many things need to be aligned,

And the words are always to be refined.

I embody perfection that wrecks me with dread in my mind.

-losing my mind

SHEREEN CHRISTINA

#96 WAVES

Swaying of spirit,

Back and forth, but never in the right direction.

The thoughts imitate the waves,

Never in one place for long,

In its own flow,

Nor high nor low tides,

Somewhere in between where the wind blows it to
the side.

Keeping it in mind and not letting it out, thundering,

Because it will be flooded with questions bothering,

Vague, the sounds formed by pondering.

Just like the waves, the mind plays in wandering.

-dwelling

SHEREEN CHRISTINA

#97 KID

It is wild or maybe weird,

That my words always disappeared.

I was never cleared;

The questions that remain unanswered.

Assuming I were skilled,

Never fulfilled,

The way I lived as a kid.

-odd childhood

SHEREEN CHRISTINA

#98 STABLE

Hanging onto the wall of hope,

Oh, I should not give up in the middle of a dark slope.

Pain is inevitable,

Even if the ache is unbearable,

Force of belief brings light to the invisible.

Upon reflection, I can become able,

Leaving behind the trouble to be stable.

-optimistic

SHEREEN CHRISTINA

#99 WARZONE

Similar sights view me tight, thinking I am a beacon of light,

No way! I am not right. I say it aloud every night,

I might write, but my mind continues to fight,

It brings quite a bite to my soul of black and white,

I will never be bright, despite being noticed with delight.

The spirit that glides in sorrow, I will not be alright.

-cold feet

SHEREEN CHRISTINA

#100 I GOT THIS

Inside my head, it rumbles,

Yearning in the midst of the troubles,

And my heart stumbles,

The uncertainty of life's symbols,

In every way, I fumble to escape; my thoughts crumble.

I got this! I got this! I mumble.

-puzzling mind

SHEREEN CHRISTINA
SHEREEN CHRISTINA
200

#101 REAL ME

Sometimes we believe we need someone to ease the pain of our loneliness.

In reality, we need to just sit by ourselves, and in silence, listen to the heartbeat that rings like a clock ticks.

Seeing the true us in the most intimate and vulnerable way.

We assume we require someone's presence when we merely desire their existence.

It is not a need but a want.

Perhaps sit by yourself and get to know the real you before the world gives its point of view.

-who am I?

"Poetry is when an emotion has found its thought and the thought has found words."

– Robert Frost –